Dr. Emmett Cooper, age 21, teaching a child the Bible one-on-one outside of Jerusalem near the Mount of Olives in May of 1974.

The HoneyWord Hexagon Logo EXPLAINED

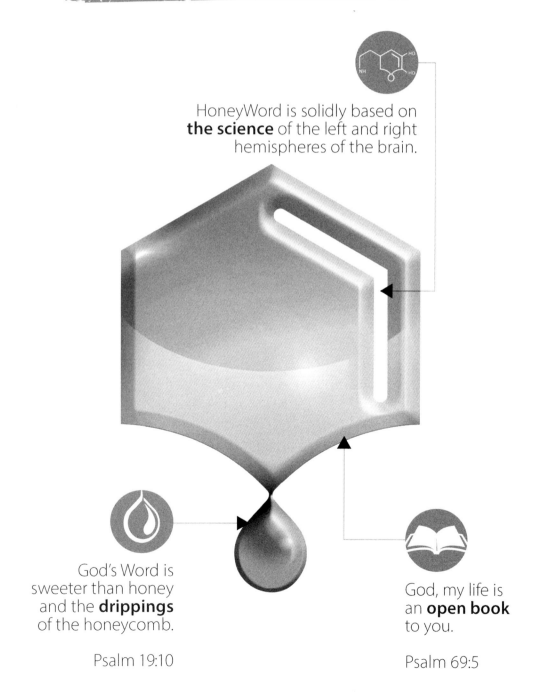

HoneyWord is solidly based on **the science** of the left and right hemispheres of the brain.

God's Word is sweeter than honey and the **drippings** of the honeycomb.

Psalm 19:10

God, my life is an **open book** to you.

Psalm 69:5

Also by Dr. Emmett Cooper

HoneyWord Bible

HoneyWord Make-it-Stick Devotions

HoneyWord Click & Stick Playing Cards

28 Days to New Life

Praise for Dr. Emmett Cooper's
HoneyWord Way of Learning

"Dr. Emmett Cooper's HoneyWord passes on the priceless legacy of Scripture to the kids in your life, whether at home, church, or school."

— **Franklin Graham**
President, Samaritan's Purse

"HoneyWord puts the spiritual cookies on the lower shelf."

— **John Maxwell**
Founder, Maxwell Leadership

"The HoneyWord Way of Learning the Bible is a breath of fresh air for all God's people everywhere."

— **Chris Hodges**
Senior Pastor, Church of the Highlands

"HoneyWord is the greatest thing that's ever happened to me. Except for Jesus."

— **Krystina Rice**
5th Grader

Copyright © 2024 by Dr. Emmett Cooper

All rights reserved.

The purpose of copyright is to encourage and protect writers and artists who produce unique and creative works that enrich our lives.

No portion of this book may be reproduced, stored in a retrieval system, or transmitted in any form or by any means — electronic, mechanical, photocopy, recording, scanning, or other — except for brief quotations in critical reviews or articles, without the prior written permission of the publisher. Any such use outside of the above stated boundaries is illegal, and a theft of the author's intellectual property.

Published in Birmingham, Alabama, by HoneyWord Publishing, HoneyWord.org.

The HoneyWord name, logo design, trademarks, lesson slogans for all 52 lessons, images, visual concepts, devotional content, Click-ers, Stick-ers, Tick-ers, the three Click-Stick-Tick bee images as well as all three phrases of the 3-Step wording of The HoneyWord Way method, all design graphics, and any and all other related elements are the intellectual property of HoneyWord Farms, LLC. The inside images were created with the assistance of Adobe Firefly. All rights reserved. 2004, 2008, 2016, 2023, 2024.

Unless otherwise indicated, all Scripture quotations are taken from the Holy Bible, New Living Translation, copyright © 1996, 2004. Used by permission of Tyndale House Publishers, Inc., Carol Stream, Illinois 60188. All rights reserved.

ISBN 979-8-9910656-0-3

Printed in the U.S.A.

HoneyWord

Red & Yellow, Black & White

All are Equal in His Sight

COLORING BOOK

Dr. Emmett Cooper
Creator of the HoneyWord Bible

HoneyWord Publishing
Birmingham, AL

Contents

Here's to the Crazy Ones	14
Crazy Offer	15
The HoneyWord Way in a Nutshell	16
52 Stick-ers Alphabetized	141

Here's to the **Crazy Ones**

"**Here's to the crazy ones.** The misfits. The rebels. The troublemakers. The round pegs in the square holes. The ones who see things differently. They're not fond of rules. And they have no respect for the status quo.

You can quote them, disagree with them, glorify or vilify them. About the only thing you can't do is ignore them. Because they change things. They push the human race forward.

And while some may see them as the crazy ones, we see genius. **Because the people who are crazy enough to think they can change the world are the ones who do.**"

Apple Computer's "Think Different" commercial, 1997

Crazy Offer

Since you're holding this book in your hands, and reading this sentence with your eyes, you're probably **one of those "crazy" passionate believers**, like us, who's tried everything to get your kid to fall in love with the Bible.

You just can't find anything that works. Until now.

We're so confident you'll love HoneyWord's spiritual results in your life, that we are offering you this money back guarantee. If for any reason, at any time, you're not flat out thrilled with how HoneyWord accelerates your heart-felt connection to Jesus, just mail this book back with your receipt and we'll refund your money in full.

The format of this life-changing book is super simple:

1. First, read the Bible verse, preferably out loud.

2. Read the short devotion to better understand the life application meaning of that verse.

3. Notice how HoneyWord spotlights **one word** of **one verse** of Scripture, **wraps it in rhyme**, and makes it **click & stick** for a lifetime through a picture called a Stick-er.

4. Ask God to personally activate any given HoneyWord Lesson in your life by "randomly" causing you to run across that exact Stick-er in your everyday life.

5. Use the right-hand page of each of these 52 lessons to journal how God answered your prayer.

We'd love to hear how this little book has increased your intimacy with God, and your love for His Word. Please send your **thoughts** and **stories** to us at **info@HoneyWord.org**.

The HoneyWord Way in a Nutshell

I want to feel God's **smile** as a life style.

*May the Lord **smile** on you.*
Numbers 6:25

I yearn to learn how my heart can **burn** for God.

*Didn't our hearts **burn** within us as Jesus explained the Scriptures to us?*
Luke 24:32

But to hear God's **Voice**, I have to make a choice,

*If you faithfully listen to the **Voice** of God…*
Deuteronomy 28:1

and say Yes!
to His cookbook
for **success.**

*Study this Book,
meditate on it day
and night for success.*
Joshua 1:8

Then as I dig big,
and fill my tank on His riverbank,
I'll find myself submarining for deep **meaning**
more and more.

*"In the future your children will ask,
'What do these stones **mean**?'"*
Joshua 4:21

Once the meaning clicks in my **Click**-er,
and I stick it to a **Stick**-er,

The Memory Pro behind the **rainbow**, makes me a charter member of those knowing how to **remember**.

*When I see the **rainbow** in the clouds, I will **remember**.*
Genesis 9:16

I love
The HoneyWord Way
of eating a Big Bowl of God's **Scroll**
every day.

*The voice said to me,
"Eat this scroll."*
Ezekiel 3:1

HoneyWord wraps God's Word in **rhyme**, and makes it click & stick for a **lifetime**.

Train up children in The HoneyWord **Way**,
Even when they're old, it'll still be clicking & sticking.

*Train up a child in the **way** he should go,
Even when he is old he will not depart from it."*
Proverb 22:6

With HoneyWord I Can Race
to the Right Place

In the days of Jesus, the New Testament had not been written yet. The Old Testament had been written on scrolls that were rolled up. It took stacks and stacks of them to hold the entire Old Testament. So when the scroll of Isaiah the prophet was handed to Jesus, how did he know where to **find** the words he wanted to read?

He had learned God's Word so well that he had no trouble finding just the right verse at just the right time. These HoneyWord Lessons will help you do the very same thing. As you learn the book and chapter location of more and more HoneyWords, you'll be able to find the truth you need for any situation you face.

The more you let these HoneyWords click in your Click-er, stick to a Stick-er, and tick in your Tick-er, the more quickly you'll be able to race to the right place every time.

Read Luke 4:17-18 NLT

*The scroll of Isaiah the prophet was handed to him. He unrolled the scroll and **found the place** where this was written: "The Spirit of the Lord is upon me…."*

Jesus Holds Me Tight
Like a Kite

After you do something that isn't right, do you wonder if you're still a member of God's family? John wanted all who believe in Jesus to know that Satan can't pull us away from our forever family. No one can separate you from the love of Jesus (see Romans 8:35). Not even your own sin.

Before you placed your faith in Christ, you were like a kite on the ground with no strength to fly. Then it was as if Jesus picked you up, tied a long unbreakable string around your heart, and set you aloft. He will never let you go. He permanently **holds you tight**, so enjoy the flight. You're on your way up, up, up to heaven, and that's worth hollering about with everything you've got.

Read 1 John 5:18 NLT
*We know that God's children do not make a practice of sinning, for God's Son **holds them securely**, and the evil one cannot touch them.*

No Work-ey
No Turkey

Many of the Thessalonians kept thinking, "If Christ is coming back any second, why work or do anything at all?" And many of them began sitting on the sidelines of life. They quit their jobs, and they even quit their chores. So Paul had to remind them that daily duties are just a fact of life.

Every day somebody has to walk the dog, feed the cat, set the table, take out the trash, and clean the bathroom. Are you helping out around the house? If not, learn from Paul's letter to the Thessalonians: "No work-ey, no turkey." In other words, if you don't pull your own weight, others shouldn't have to pull it for you. Stand up. Chip in. Do your part. **Work.**

Read 2 Thessalonians 3:10 NLT

*Even while we were with you, we gave you this command: "Those unwilling to **work** will not get to eat."*

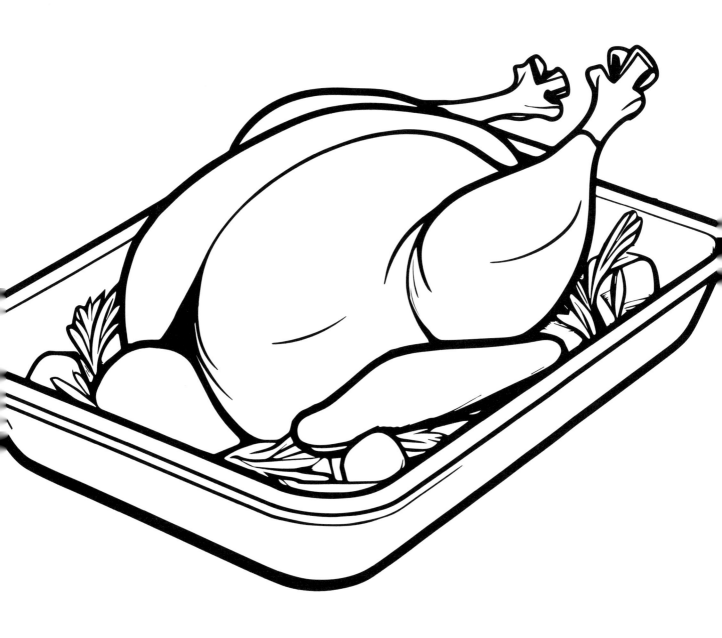

I Carry God's Map
in My Thinking Cap

When Jeremiah mailed this letter to God's people in Babylon, Daniel was already there. As a young man, Daniel studied and followed God's Word like a map, so that it directed all his thinking, and helped him to make wise decisions.

One day as an old man, Daniel just happened to be studying this chapter of Jeremiah (see Daniel 9:1-2), and learned about God's plan to bring His people home after 70 years of having to live in another country.

Like Daniel, you also can learn about God's **plans** for you. But you've got to first, stick God's Word—His map—inside your thinking cap, or it will never happen.

Read Jeremiah 29:11 NLT

*"I know the plans I have for you," says the Lord. "They are **plans** for good and not for disaster, to give you a future and a hope."*

God is the Memory Pro
Behind the Rainbow

After the worldwide flood, God showed up and had a one-way chat with Noah. He promised to never again flood the entire earth with water.

When He tied His "never again" promise to the **rainbow**, He literally showed Noah and his family, and us, how memory works. Like God, whenever you want to remember anything, especially His Word, the Bible—tie that truth to an everyday item. Then when you randomly **see** that "Click-er" again, you will automatically **remember** the exact meaning you tied to it.

God practices what He preaches. He made his rainbow promise stick in His mind (and ours) by tying it to a symbol exactly the way He commands us to teach in Deuteronomy 6:8. God is the Memory Pro behind the rainbow. Learn and remember like Him.

Read Genesis 9:13,16 NLT

I have placed my rainbow in the clouds. It is the sign of my covenant with you and with all the earth… ***When I see the rainbow*** *in the clouds,* ***I will remember*** *the eternal covenant between God and every living creature on earth.*

In the Beginning, God's Call
Got the Ball . . . Rolling

Did you know that a very long time ago nothing was around except God? Then, when God decided the time was just right, He created everything.

God created the sun, the moon, and the stars. He made the little **ball** we live on called Planet Earth, and He made every living thing on Earth. He also created the sky above and the oceans below. God made the call to create every fish, bird, and animal. When it was time to make people, God made that **call**, too. None of this was an accident.

In the big beginning, only God was big enough to make the **call** that got the **ball** rolling. He is the only one big and powerful enough to keep it going, day after day.

Read Genesis 1:1 NLT

*In the beginning **God created** the heavens and the earth.*

God Made Me Bloom
in My Mother's Womb

Sooner or later you'll hear people ask questions like these: When does a baby become a real person? Is it during the first month inside its mother? How about after the sixth month? Or maybe only after it's born? Questions like these are missing the point, because He feels the same way about you as He did about Jeremiah.

God knew all about you and loved you even before He made you bloom in your mother's **womb**, and He will remain your best friend throughout your entire life. After that, He wants to spend all of eternity with you. Always remember that God knows and loves everything about you, from womb to tomb, and beyond.

Jeremiah 1:5 NLT

*I knew you before I formed you in your mother's **womb**.*
Before you were born I set you apart and appointed you
as my prophet to the nations.

Red and Yellow, Black and White
All are Equal in His Sight

We humans tend to make a big fuss over color. Some people eat only red apples—they won't touch green or yellow ones. Some folks dye their hair black, and others dye it blonde. When it comes to differences in clothing, we look like a field of multicolored flowers.

If God had a middle name, it could be "Variety." We see it everywhere throughout His creation. But unfortunately, some of us can't see how this applies to the color of people's skin. In fact, many people don't like anyone who doesn't look just like they do.

But God doesn't think like that. Red, yellow, black, white, men, women, boys, girls, old and young, all are beautiful … and totally **equal** … in His sight. God created all the colors of the rainbow and loves every one of them. You can, too.

Galatians 3:28 NLT
*There is no longer Jew or Gentile, slave or free, male and female. For you are **all one** in Christ Jesus.*

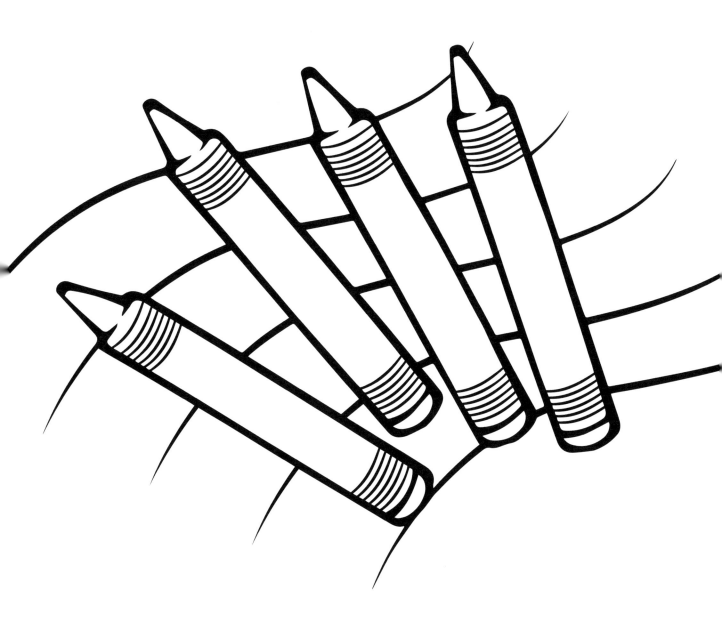

All My Troubles
are Like Bubbles

Troubles? Paul had them by the truckload. He was unjustly jailed multiple times, flogged, slandered, cursed, and beaten with rods three times. He was shipwrecked, robbed, hungry, homeless, and experienced constant death threats. The list goes on and on. His suffering was up close, personal, and intense–almost daily.

God taught Paul that faithfulness during one pound of temporary suffering down here, gets converted into a hundred tons of permanent reward up there. That's what kept Paul going, and it's the same for you and me.

As you learn to fix your gaze on the eternal, God will reveal how all your **troubles** are like bubbles ready to burst. The very worst things in life down here will eventually give way to the joys of heaven up there.

2 Corinthians 4:17-18 NLT

*We don't look at the **troubles** we can see now; rather, we fix our gaze on things that cannot be seen. For the things we see now will soon be gone, but the things we cannot see will last forever.*

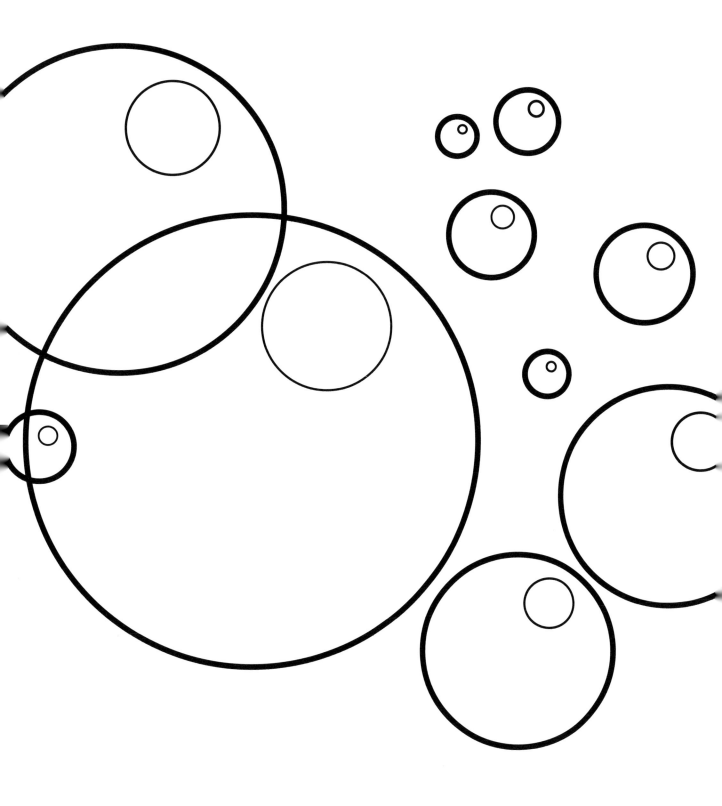

Jesus is the Bread
That Keeps Me Fed

After multiplying a handful of food and feeding 5,000, everybody got excited about the free lunch program they thought Jesus started. When they found Him again the next day, He knew they were just looking for another meal deal—and had missed the point entirely.

Yes, eating is a fact of life. If you don't eat, eventually you'll starve and die. The same is true spiritually. Just as food fills your stomach and keeps your body going, Jesus, the **Bread** of Life, gives your spirit the spiritual energy to follow God.

As you establish your new life in Christ, watch your diet. Eat the Bread of Life, and feed on Him often in God's Word. He will lead you in the way, day by day.

John 6:48 NLT
*Yes, I am the **bread** of life!*

I Can Shoot Arrows of Prayer
From Anywhere

We can pray anytime, anywhere, because God is always listening and always ready to answer. Nehemiah prayed right in the middle of a conversation, and shot a short prayer to God for help. Like a narrow arrow, it was to the point and hit the target. God heard and answered, helping Nehemiah know what to say to the king.

God loves getting showered with short prayers. The key to prayer is faith (trusting God), not the number of words. Whenever you need help, shoot short arrows of **prayer** to God. He'll get the point, and you'll get the power!

Nehemiah 2:4-5 NLT

*The king asked, "Well, how can I help you?" With a **prayer** to the God of heaven, I replied, "If it please the king, and if you are pleased with me, your servant, send me to Judah to rebuild the city."*

I Believe in God's
Perfect Weave

Weaving is the process of making cloth by crossing two sets of threads over and under each other. One set, the warp, is stretched up and down on a loom or frame. The other set, the weft, gets woven from left to right. (Get it? Weft—left!) To make cloth, a weaver threads the weft over and under the warp again and again.

God is the Master Weaver. He promises to make every up-and-down and over-and-under weave of your life **work together** for your good. Learn to believe in God's perfect weave. Tell him often, out loud, that you trust His leadership in your life, no matter what.

Romans 8:28 NLT

*We know that God causes everything to **work together** for the good of those who love God and are called according to his purpose for them.*

Two Can Do a Canoe
Better Than One

Paddling around in a canoe all by yourself isn't much fun. It's just plain hard work! The point Solomon is making in this verse is that everything goes better with a friend. Work is easier, and play is more fun. Even falling down is better, because someone's there to help you get up.

God understands our need for **friends**—in fact, he built us to need them. We really can't make it through life without them. But to get friends, you have to be a friend. Part of being a friend is taking the first step, again and again.

If you don't learn this now, you might find yourself paddling through life all alone.

Ecclesiastes 4:9 NLT
***Two** people are **better** off than **one**,*
for they can help each other succeed.

I Don't Dismiss
God's Inner Compass

Have you ever wondered how airplanes fly at night through dense fog, or how ships make it through big storms? They do it by using a compass that shows them which way they're headed, by magnetically pointing them to the North Pole.

Pilots and sea captains aren't the only ones who use a compass. Campers, hunters, and even car drivers use them to get from one place to another.

All of us are born with special compasses in our hearts that know how to get a bearing on God's true north. Our internal compass steers us in the right direction, and it lets us know when we get off track. Whenever you're tempted to **dismiss** God's inner compass, don't push the truth away, follow it carefully and stay on course.

Ecclesiastes 4:9 NLT

*God shows his anger from heaven against all sinful, wicked people who **suppress** the truth by their wickedness. They know the truth about God because he has made it obvious to them.*

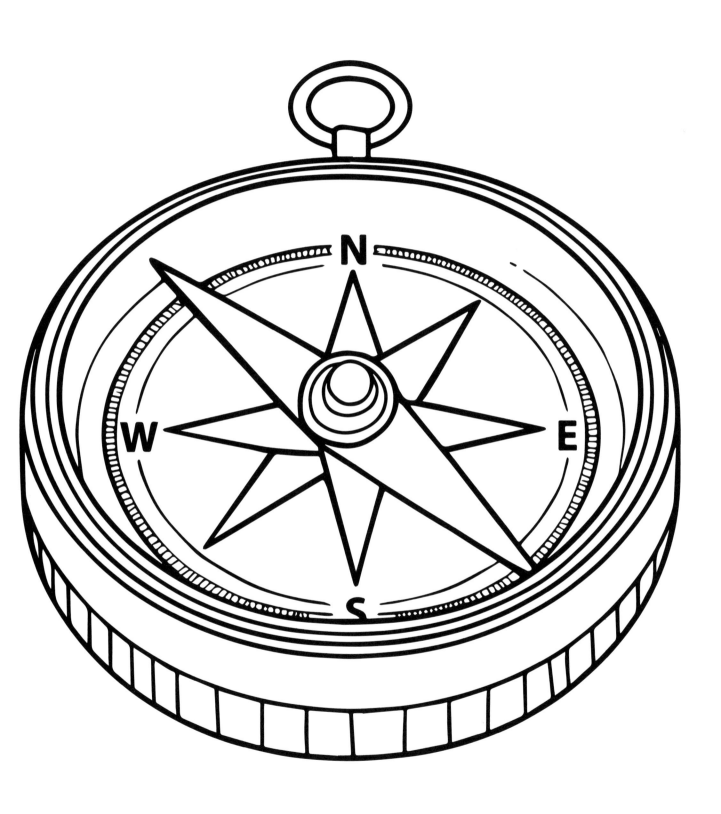

I Love the Dove
From Above

The baptism of Jesus, by John the Baptist, was a special event. God's voice from heaven said, "You are my dearly loved Son, and you bring me great joy." As Jesus came up out of the water, the Spirit of God came down on Him in the form of a **dove**.

But why a gentle dove? Why not a fierce eagle instead? No one knows for sure, but we can guess. Like a dove, the Holy Spirit is very sweet and tenderhearted. In Ephesians 4:30 we are told not to make the Holy Spirit sad. And 1 Thessalonians 5:19 clearly says that we are not to choke out the Holy Spirit.

You see, the Spirit is so kind and peace-loving that He works at our invitation only. He's always with us, but we don't always follow Him. So love the Dove from above, and let Him have His way in your life.

Mark 1:10 NLT

*As Jesus came up out of the water, he saw the heavens splitting apart and the Holy Spirit descending on him like a **dove**.*

I'm Knit to Fit
for Life

Have you ever thought about how God forms a baby inside its mother? If so, you're not the only one. King David thought about it too, and as he did, he realized that he didn't know how to explain it. He compared it to knitting, which was something he did understand. He knew that when someone **knits** a scarf or sweater, the person does it by hand. It's a personal gift that takes lots of time, skill and attention to detail.

In the same personal, careful way, God forms every baby. Only God can make a baby and only God could have made you. He lovingly made you stitch by stitch. You're not a mistake. You are a wonderful miracle. We know it's true because God says so!

Psalm 139:13-14 NLT

*You made all the delicate, inner parts of my body and **knit** me together in my mother's womb.*

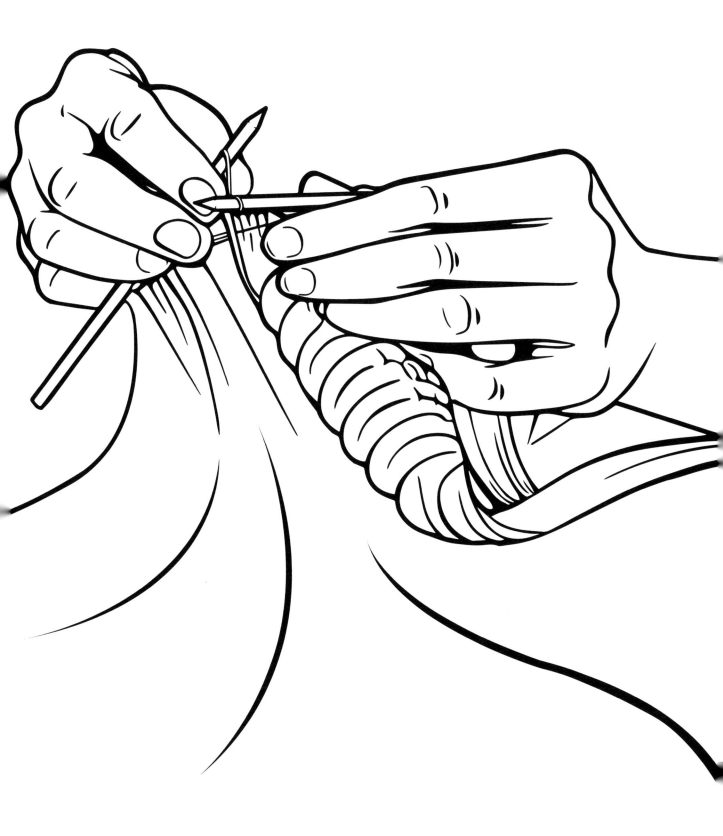

His Soap
Gives Me Hope

Soap comes in many forms: bars, flakes, grains, liquids and tablets, and we use it for cleaning all kinds of things: hands, hair, clothes and dishes. Daily bathing with soap keeps dirt and body oils from clogging the pores of our skin.

In this verse, John reminds us that everybody also needs spiritual **cleansing**. But if we want God to forgive us and clean away our sins, we first have to confess them. That simply means sincerely praying a one-sentence prayer: "I was wrong, and I'm sorry." Then God forgives us because His son Jesus has already dies for our sins.

That one requirement doesn't seem like too big of a deal, but you'd be amazed at the number of people who refuse to come clean with God. Don't be like them. Admit your dirt, and then let Jesus' soap scrub you clean and give you hope.

1 John 1:9 NLT

*If we confess our sins to him, he is faithful and just to forgive us of our sins and to **cleanse** us from all wickedness.*

I Dwell
on What's Behind the Shell

TV shows, movies, and magazine covers try to show us how our outside shells should look. If we've got the right face, body, and clothes, we have **"The Look"** and we're cool. If we don't, we're out. It's nothing new.

When Samuel dropped by Jesse's house to anoint the second King of Israel, the minute he saw Jesse's son Eliab, he thought, "Whoa, this is the guy!". But Samuel was wrong. While Eliab had "The Look," David had "The Heart." So God told Samuel to anoint David.

Your outside shell is what people see first, but with God, what you're like inside is a much bigger deal. Don't worry about the shell, just dwell on what's behind it—in yourself and others.

1 Samuel 16:6-7 NLT

*Samuel took one look at Eliab and thought, "Surely this is the Lord's anointed!" But the Lord said to Samuel, "Don't judge by his appearance or height, for I have rejected him. The Lord doesn't see things the way you see them. People judge by **outward appearance**, but the Lord looks at the heart."*

God Came Down
and Gave me a Crown

As a shepherd, David had plenty of time to think about life, God, and the universe. This psalm is about one of those moments David had one night while his sheep were sleeping. As he looked up into the heavens, he started thinking about how big and awesome God is, and how small and unimportant people seem to be.

Then he thought about the place of high honor God has given His people in the world He created. You see, we're not some unimportant pieces of dust floating in space. We are the most important part of God's entire creation. That's why He **crowned** us with glory and honor.

Doesn't that make you feel special? It should, because God created people, including you, to rule over the rest of His creation.

Psalm 8:4-5 NLT

*What are mere mortals that you should think about them, human beings that you should care for them? Yet you made them only a little lower than God and **crowned** them with glory and honor.*

I Can Eat-zza
Greasy, Cheesy Pizza

The religious leaders back in Jesus' day had rules on top of rules. Don't do this. Don't do that. Don't eat this! Do eat that. Now, there's nothing wrong with rules. We all need them. But Jesus knew these people loved to keep rules more than they loved knowing God.

The key to a clean heart, then and now, is not what you put into your stomach. What's important is what you do with evil thoughts that come up out of your heart. You need to bring those thoughts to Jesus, so He can wash them out and keep your friendship with God fresh and clean.

You can choose to eat or not **eat-zza** greasy, cheesy pizza. But you can't make your heart pure for God. Only Jesus can do that.

Mark 7:19-21 NLT

*"Food doesn't go into your heart, but only passes through the stomach"... (By saying this, [Jesus] declared that **every kind of food** is acceptable in God's eyes.) And then he added, "It is what comes from inside that defiles you."*

I Won't Steel
Even an Orange Peel

Maybe you've heard a news story about someone who robbed a bank and took other people's money. Perhaps a person in your town stole a car. You might think stealing big things is worse than stealing little things, but stealing is stealing.

Some people start taking a penny here and a nickel there. They keep taking what isn't theirs until they take more and more things. You don't have to start that habit. God is very clear about stealing. One of His commandments says, "You must not **steal**." This means even little things.

Whenever you're tempted to steal something that belongs to someone else, even if it's as small as an **orange peel**, don't take it. Leave it alone. Then you'll be pleasing God.

Deuteronomy 5:19 NLT
*You must not **steal**.*

God is Able
to Turn the Tables

Haman created an evil plan that almost killed Mordecai and the entire Jewish race. But just in the nick of time, God used Esther, the young Jewish queen of Persia, to turn the tables on Haman. He was killed instead of Mordecai, and all the Jewish people were saved.

This dramatic **turn around** shows how quickly God can change things. God is good at last-minute rescue operations. What are you facing that looks and feels hopeless? If you keep bringing it to God in prayer, in His own time and in His own way, He will turn the tables for you.

But between now and then, trust that He has a good plan that He will reveal and unfold. At just the right time, He will **take back** what has been stolen from you, and **give it** to you with delight.

Esther 8:1-2 NLT

*On that same day King Xerxes gave the property of Haman, the enemy of the Jews, to Queen Esther. Then ... the king took off his signet ring—which he had **taken back** from Haman— and **gave it** to Mordecai.*

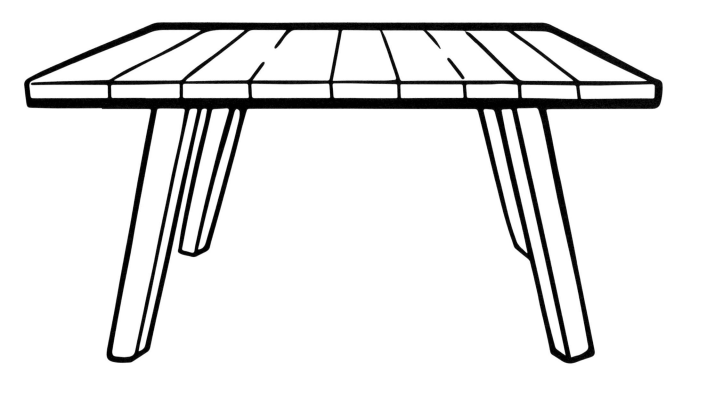

I Sin
When I Judge on the Basis of Skin

In Persia, the Jewish people stood out like zebras in a herd of black horses. Everything about them seemed different, the way they looked, the way they talked, even the way they worshipped.

Haman, the king's top man, didn't like their differences one bit, so he decided to kill the Jewish people. Isn't that sad? It's always wrong to hurt people for being different.

We are all beautiful, and created in God's image. Don't look down on people because of their **skin** color, the clothes they wear, or the way they talk. It's a sin, and it makes God really sad.

Esther 3:6 NLT

*[Haman] had learned of Mordecai's nationality, so he decided it was not enough to lay hands on Mordecai alone. Instead, he looked for a way to **destroy all the Jews** throughout the entire empire of Xerxes.*

I Find Rest
in His Nest

Every bird builds a special kind of nest. Some of these nests look neat, while others look messy. Wrens make tiny nests, while eagles form huge ones.

But every nest is a safe, warm home for a family of birds. It's where they eat, sleep, and grow up. When the baby birds are ready to fly the coop, it becomes a launching pad for their first flight.

Think of the arms of Jesus as a warm cozy nest, where you can find rest from anything that seems hard or makes you feel bad. Do you get tired or worry a lot? Crawl into Jesus' nest, and let Him teach you how to **rest**.

Matthew 11:28-29 NLT

*Then Jesus said, "Come to me, all of you who are weary and carry heavy burdens, and I will give you **rest**. Take my yoke upon you. Let me teach you, because I am humble and gentle at heart, and you will find rest for your souls."*

I Use My Shoes
to Share the Good News

Have you ever thought about all the different kinds of shoes in the world? We've got baseball, basketball, soccer, tennis, even jogging shoes. And then, there are sandals, clogs, sneakers, loafers, moccasins, boots, and bedroom slippers. The list could probably go on forever, but all **shoes** have one main purpose: to protect our **feet** while we're getting to where we're going.

As Christians, we too have a primary purpose, which is to share the Good News about Jesus wherever our feet and shoes take us. You see, people wearing shoes that go and share the gospel are beautiful in the eyes of God. Some beautiful person brought it to you, and you can take it to others.

Romans 10:15 NLT

*How will anyone go and tell them without being sent? That is why the Scriptures say, "How beautiful are the **feet** of messengers who bring good news!"*

I Love God's Honey
More Than Money

In Psalm 19 David made a big list of good things that come from obeying God's Word: protection, joy, wisdom, light, and insight. Then he said two amazing things: God's Word is way better than tons of money, and it's so sweet to the soul that it tastes better than honey. You might not believe that now, but one day you will.

As you choose to follow God, you'll find that His **honey** (the Bible) is the sweetest thing in life. You'll want to taste more and more of it, and it will be a greater help than any amount of money.

Psalm 19:9-10 NLT

Reverence for the Lord is pure, lasting forever. The laws of the Lord are true; each one is fair. They are more desirable than gold, even the finest gold. They are sweeter than honey, even **honey** *dripping from the comb.*

Jesus Steers
Through Listening Ears

Voice recognition software has taken the world by storm. Spoken words can magically appear on the screens of computers and smart devices. Better yet, Siri, Cortana, Google or Alexa—the Fab Four of voice-activated digital assistants, can somehow literally hear our voice and do what we say. It's amazing, efficient and effective.

Isaiah 42:3 prophetically described Jesus as one who will not shout you down or ream you out. He's gentle and humble in heart. His yoke is easy, and His voice is quiet—almost silent. That's why it's so easy to miss it.

Commit early on in your Christian life to unplug daily from the artificial intelligence of our noisy culture. Get quiet, pray, and incline your heart. Read the Word, and tune in. Jesus steers through **listening** ears.

John 10:27 NLT

*My sheep **listen** to my voice; I know them, and they follow me.*

For Every Dollar
God Gets a Dime Every Time

Old Testament Levites, like pastors today, were paid from the tithes of God's people. So, did the Levites have to tithe? Yep, all God's people, then and now, are to give God one dime for every 10 dimes—every dollar they get.

Really, everything belongs to God. He's placed what we have in our care and only asks for a **tenth** of it back. That's so easy, you'd think all Christians would do it all the time, but they don't because we all struggle with selfishness.

Don't fall into that trap. God promises to give big-time blessings to anyone who faithfully tithes. Start **tithing** today. Give God one dime every time you get one dollar.

Numbers 18:26 NLT

*Give these instructions to the Levites: When you receive from the people of Israel the **tithes** I have assigned as your allotment, give a **tenth** of the tithes you receive—a tithe of the tithe— to the Lord as a sacred offering.*

I'm in the Gang
Throwing God's Boomerang

There are many places in the Bible where God tells us that what we give has everything to do with what we get back. It's like using a boomerang.

Invented thousands of years ago, the boomerang is a flat, curved piece of wood that can be thrown, so it returns to the person who threw it. Isn't that amazing? But, even more amazing is how giving to others follows the same flight plan.

Whatever we give will circle around and someday come back to us. Are you in the gang throwing God's boomerang? If so, get ready to receive. Whatever you throw, good or bad, God will one day **boomerang** it back to you.

Ecclesiastes 11:1 NLT
Send your grain across the seas, and in time,
*profits will **flow back** to you.*

Like a Yo-Yo
I Get My Go-Go From the Hand of God

The yo-yo may have been invented as a hunting weapon thousands of years ago in the Philippines. There's also evidence that the ancient Greeks played with this toy. Over the years, many fun tricks have been developed for the yo-yo, from "Loop the Loop" to "Walk the Dog" to "Rock the Baby." But a yo-yo can only go-go when it's attached to a hand. By itself it's totally useless.

In the same way, we're spiritually powerless without God. However, when we place ourselves in His hands, His mighty **power** accomplishes more through us than we could ever hope.

Be like a yo-yo, get your **go-go** from the hand of God. Then get ready to watch God use you to "Loop-the-Loop" and "Walk-the-Dog" all over your world.

Ephesians 3:20 NLT

*Now all glory to God, who is able, through his mighty **power** at work within us, to accomplish infinitely more than we might ask or think.*

I Like Submarining
for Deep Meaning in the Word

Some of the first submarines were used in the American Civil War. These amazing machines are used not only by our navy, but by scientists who explore deep water. Small robot-controlled submarines with cameras were used to explore the shipwrecked Titanic, others found fish thought to no longer exist.

Just like explorers in an ocean, we can "submarine" into God's Word and find answers to things we wonder about. Exploring God's Word is an adventure you can start now, and enjoy for the rest of your life.

The deeper you "submarine" for **meaning** in God's Word, the more you'll discover there is to find. Dive in!

Joshua 4:21-22 NLT

*Then Joshua said to the Israelites, "In the future your children will ask, 'What do these stones **mean**?' Then you can tell them, 'This is where the Israelites crossed the Jordan on dry ground.'"*

I'm Willing to Go Out On a Limb
for Him

If we compare trusting God to climbing a tree, we could say that God is always calling us to climb out farther on a limb. God makes sure that we will never outclimb or outgrow our need for trust.

Ruth is a beautiful picture of someone who kept trusting God during the worst time of her life. When everything within her wanted to climb down and quit, she kept climbing up and trusting.

Are you climbing up to God in faith, or are you climbing down away from Him in fear? Be willing to "**go out on a limb**" for God by trusting Him. He will calm your fears and meet your needs. That's a promise!

Ruth 2:11 NLT

"Yes, I know," Boaz replied. "But I also know about everything you have done for your mother-in-law since the death of your husband. ***I have heard how you left*** *your father and mother and your own land to live here among complete strangers."*

When I Hit a Brick Wall
God is Who I Call

As slaves, the people of God were "up against a brick wall." Pharaoh gave them the impossible task of making the same number of bricks each day, even though they now also had to find their own straw.

At times, we too, run into what seems like a **brick** wall. We lose a pet. Our parents fight and talk about getting a divorce. A friend gets a serious illness. Whenever life makes us feel like we're up against a brick wall, it may seem that we're all alone. But we're not—God is with us. He promises to hear our prayers and put peace back in our hearts.

Have you hit a brick wall? Call out to God, and He will help you know what to do.

Exodus 5:13 NLT
*The Egyptian slave drivers continued to push hard. "Meet your daily quota of **bricks**, just as you did when we provided you with straw!" they demanded.*

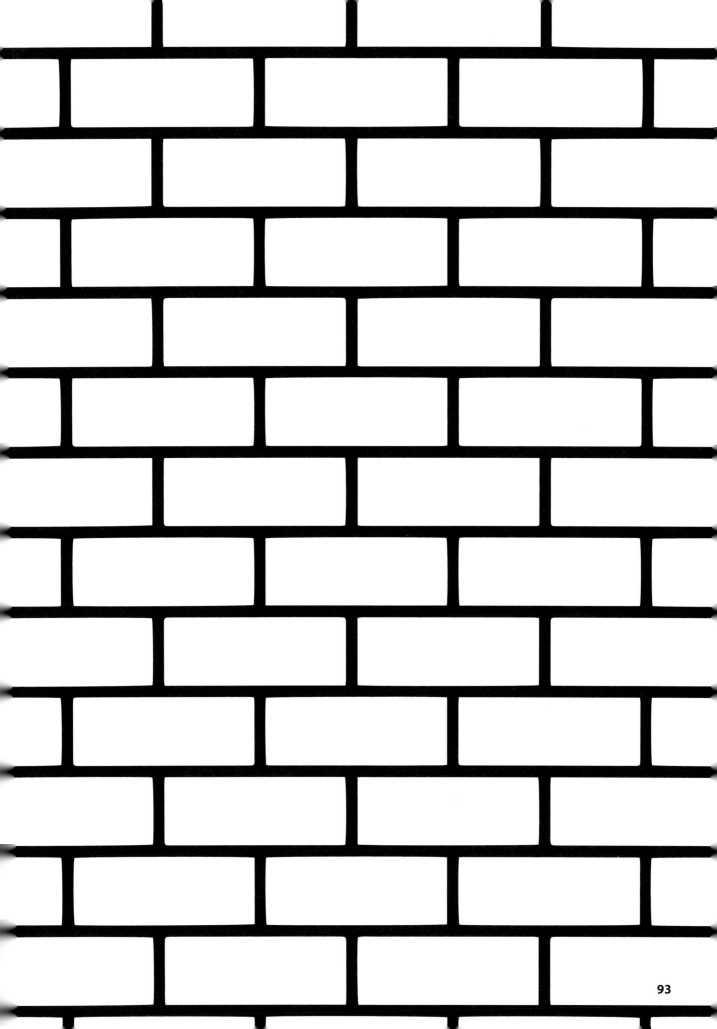

I Only Watch
Top-Notch TV

TVs are everywhere. There's both bad and good stuff on TV, but sometimes you have to look hard to find the good.

It would be interesting to ask King David (who wrote this Psalm) about today's TV programs. We know he would "refuse to look at anything **vile** and **vulgar**." Without going into a lot of detail about the meaning of these two V words, it's safe to say the following words could take their place: evil and defiling.

Would David have watched anything like that? Psalm 101 tells us no way! Be like David, and only watch what's top-notch.

Psalm 101:2-3 NLT

I will lead a life of integrity in my own home.
*I will refuse to look at anything **vile** and **vulgar**.*

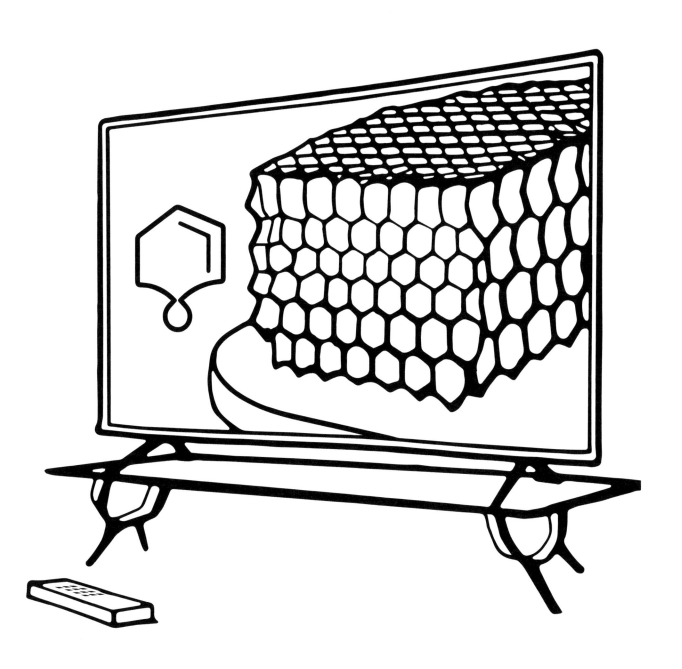

I'm Diving Deep
for Treasure to Keep

Many years ago, a treasure hunter named Mel Fisher began looking for a Spanish ship full of gold and silver treasures. He believed it had sunk somewhere off the coast of Florida.

For sixteen years he searched for it. One day he found it. It's now on record as the single largest treasure ever found, worth hundreds of millions of dollars.

But even that treasure is nothing compared to the value of God's Word! If you search for wisdom in the Bible, you'll find a super rich life of walking with God. Dive deep for God's treasure. It's the only **treasure** you can keep in this life and the next!

Proverbs 2:2-4 NLT

*Tune your ears to wisdom, and concentrate on understanding. Cry out for insight, and ask for understanding. Search for them as you would for silver; seek them like hidden **treasures**.*

My Sword
is the Word of the Lord

The "Word of God" in this verse refers to the Bible, the written Word of God. However, in Revelation 19:13 the "Word of God" is a name for Jesus, The Man, coming back in glory at the end of this age. Collectively, therefore these two passages make it clear that Jesus, the living Word, is the same as Jesus, the written Word. They are one and the same.

The writer of Hebrews goes on to compare this written Word of God to an extremely sharp sword that cuts. That same description is used in Revelation 19:15 where we see a sharp **sword** coming out of the mouth of Jesus.

Here's the point: whatever comes from Jesus, whether it's written or spoken, will always cut to the bone of your life. But like a loving surgeon, God only cuts what He intends to heal.

Hebrews 4:12 NLT

*The Word of God is alive and powerful. It is sharper than the sharpest two-edged **sword**, cutting between soul and spirit, between joint and marrow. It exposes our innermost thoughts and desires.*

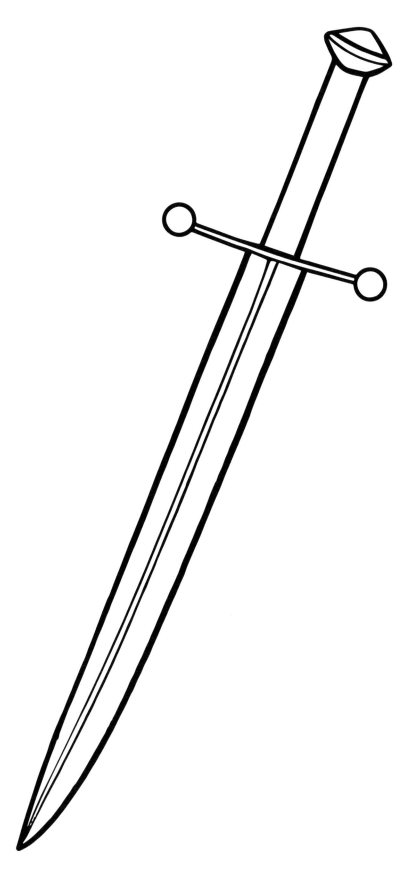

I Won't Break Out in a Rash
if I Take Out the Trash

The job of chopping and stacking wood doesn't sound too spiritual, but it needed to be done to keep the fire burning on the altar. So Nehemiah assigned the job to the priests and Levites who worked at the Temple.

Daily chores are just a fact of life. Every day somebody's got to make the bed, pick up the towels, walk the dog, feed the cat, set the table, load the dishwasher, and on and on. It's not a question of if the stuff has to be done, but **who** will do it.

If your **assigned task** is to take out the garbage, then do it every day. You won't break out in a rash taking out the trash. But your parents might break out in the "Hallelujah Chorus" if you do your chores faithfully and cheerfully.

Nehemiah 13:30-31 NLT

*I **assigned tasks** to the priests and Levites, making certain that each knew his work. I also made sure that the supply of wood for the altar and the first portions of the harvest were brought at the proper times.*

I Won't Let the Evil Spider
Be a Divider

Believe it or not, there are more than 34,000 known species of spiders in the world. For most of us, that's about 34,000 too many!

Spiders are sinister creatures tirelessly spinning their silk webs to catch bugs for food. Some spiders build webs so strong, they snag insects several times larger and stronger than themselves. That's why the devil could be accurately described as the "Evil Spider." He's always spinning a web of lies, hoping to deceive us Christians into believing he is much more powerful than we are—which he isn't (1 John 4:4).

Anger is one of his biggest traps. Anger, you see, is usually expressed in words. And words delivered in a single moment of rage can divide and sometimes cripple relationships for life. Don't let the slimy Evil **Spider** be a divider. Work things out before you go to bed.

Ephesians 4:26-27 NLT

*"Don't sin by letting anger control you." Don't let the sun go down while you are still angry, for anger gives a foothold to **the devil.***

I Only Shine
When I Stick to the Vine

Bananas don't grow in grocery stores, and strawberries don't sprout from plastic bins. Fruit only flows from branches attached to living plants. Apples therefore exclusively come through apple branches, peaches from peach tree branches, and grapes solely through grapevine branches. But no fruit grows on branches that have broken off.

This simple teaching of Jesus paints a powerful picture of the way things work—and don't work—in the natural, as well as the spiritual. He's the **vine**, and we are the branches. Stay connected to Him and live, or disconnect and die.

So stick to the Vine. It's the only way to shine.

John 15:5 NLT

*Yes, I am the **vine**; you are the branches. Those who remain in me, and I in them, will produce much fruit. For apart from me you can do nothing.*

I'm Sold on Giving Cold
Cups of Water

Have you ever seen a sign offering a reward for a lost pet? You have to find that animal and return it to its owner before you get the money, right? That's the way rewards work. They only come when you do what's expected of you.

The same is true with God. If we want to receive rewards from Him, we must first learn what He expects of us. This passage gives us a clue. He wants us to notice what people need and give it to them. He wants us to welcome visitors and serve them. Even if we just offer a guest a **cup of cold water**, God will see that and reward us, maybe in this life, but for sure in heaven.

Get sold on giving cold cups of water, and get ready to receive some really cool rewards.

Mark 9:41 NLT

*If anyone gives you even a **cup of water** because you belong to the Messiah, I tell you the truth, that person will surely be rewarded.*

I Handle His Candle
With Care

Have you ever heard of the word, stifle? It means to choke or murder by strangling. How can we kill God the Holy Spirit? We can't. But we can choke out the work He wants to do through us.

The Holy Spirit is all-powerful, yet He operates in our hearts so gently that He's like a flickering **candle**. Because the Spirit of God is Holy just like God the Father, He won't have anything to do with sin. The Holy Spirit never leaves you, but sin can certainly dampen His plans for you.

So handle His candle with care. Whenever you sin, admit it to God. Each time He will forgive you and ignite His flame within you once again.

1 Thessalonians 5:19 NLT

*Do not **stifle** the Holy Spirit.*

I Plunge Like a Sponge
in the Word

Sponges don't move. They pick a spot on the bottom of the ocean, latch on, lock down, and stay put. And once anchored, they spend all day every day filtering huge quantities of water, an estimated 20,000 times greater than their own volume, and cleaning up everything around them.

Back in the time of the Old Testament, the first order of business for new kings was to attach to and ground themselves on the Word of God, and not move, ever. They were to be so continuously **immersed** in God's Word, that it would constantly flow through the pores of their spiritual DNA, informing all of life. Day in and day out.

Deuteronomy 17:18-19 NLT

*When he sits on the throne as king, he must copy for himself this body of instruction on a scroll ... He must always keep that copy with him and **read it daily** as long as he lives. That way he will learn to fear the LORD his God by obeying all the terms of these instructions and decrees.*

My Words Give Life
or Cut Like a Knife

Have you ever looked closely at your tongue in the mirror?
It's kind of gross and funny looking, don't you think? It's attached to the bottom of your mouth by a shiny, tissue-thin piece of skin, and the top is a grainy-looking field of bumps called taste buds.

Somehow, when food rubs next to these bumps or liquid sloshes all over them, the brain is able to send us signals like "yum, ice cream," or "yuck, medicine."

But that's not all the tongue can do, it shapes the sounds of words that make people feel good, or make them feel bad. Kind words make people happy to be alive. Unkind words make people hurt inside. Don't use your tongue to **cut** people down. Use it to build them up, and give life to everyone around you.

Proverb 12:18 NLT
*Some people make **cutting remarks**,*
but the words of the wise bring healing.

Jesus is My Flashlight
Day and Night

Have you ever gone camping? If you're not used to it, a night in the country can be quite a shock, it's very dark without city lights. That's when a flashlight really makes a big difference. It can keep you from stumbling over a fallen tree branch on the way to the bathroom. However, when you get the munchies, your flashlight can help you find the snack bag.

Jesus tells us that He is light. When we follow Him, He lights the way in front of us just like a flashlight. Step by step, He shows us the right path to take. He also shows us things to avoid.

And one more thing: The **light** of Jesus never goes out, and never needs new batteries. He's always there, lighting the way **day** and **night**, so stick tight to Him.

John 8:12 NLT

*Jesus spoke to the people once more and said, "I am the **light** of the world. If you follow me, you won't have to walk in darkness, because you will have the light that leads to life."*

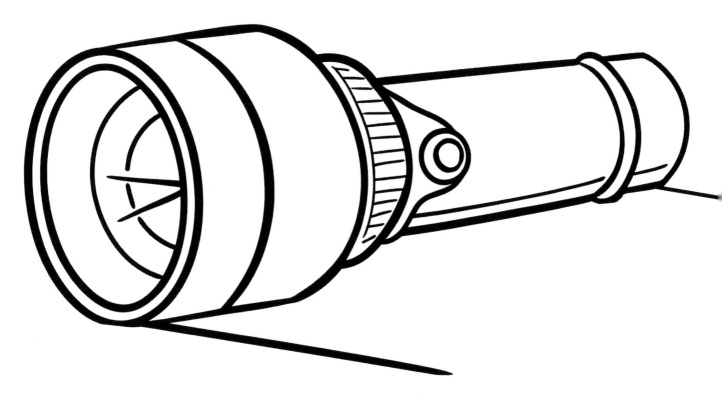

Jesus is My Rock
Around the Clock

Two men built two homes. We don't know who they were, where they came from, or what style of home they built. All we know is that one guy anchored his house to bedrock, and the other tied his to sand.

Then everything was fine. Until it wasn't. Severe storms came, as they always do, and relentlessly beat against both homes. One stood, and one collapsed. Why? Because one was cemented on purpose to immovable **rock**, while the other was carelessly wedded to watery mudslides.

As a skilled carpenter, Jesus is hammering home one simple truth: building homes and building lives are one and the same. Both require a rock-solid foundation as priority one. Let Jesus be your daily rock. He alone can uphold you around the clock.

Matthew 7:24-25 NLT

*Anyone who listens to my teaching and follows it is wise, like a person who builds a house on solid **rock**. Though the rain comes in torrents and the floodwaters rise and the winds beat against that house, it won't collapse because it is built on bedrock.*

It's Pretty Neat
How God Hits Delete

When typing or texting we all make mistakes or typos, and then delete certain letters, words, whole sentences, and even entire paragraphs of thought.

The word "delete" comes from the Latin word deletus, which means "to wipe out totally." The **delete** button, that's become indispensable to our daily digital lifestyle, has an exact parallel function in our day-to-day spiritual walk with God.

Whenever you sin in any given moment, just confess that sin to God, and then simply hit his divine delete button, Jesus, who **blots out** and totally wipes out that sin forever.

Isaiah 43:25 NLT

*I—yes, I alone—will **blot out** your sins for*

my own sake and will never think of them again.

God Plans My Plot
Dot-to-Dot

Everybody's life is a story with lots of day-to-day details. And, every story has a plot—that's the story line. Have you ever wondered how much God knows and remembers about your plot?

Did He see those bumps you got as you learned how to walk? Did He see when you first rode a bike? Was He around when you first tied your shoes? What about the times when you were alone?

The answer is YES! YES! YES! God always follows your life plot, dot-to-dot, day by day, in every way. He sees and cares about **everything** you do. Even though you can't see Him, God is always with you. In fact, your plot is his daily delight.

Psalm 37:23 NLT

The Lord directs the steps of the godly.

*He delights in **every detail** of their lives.*

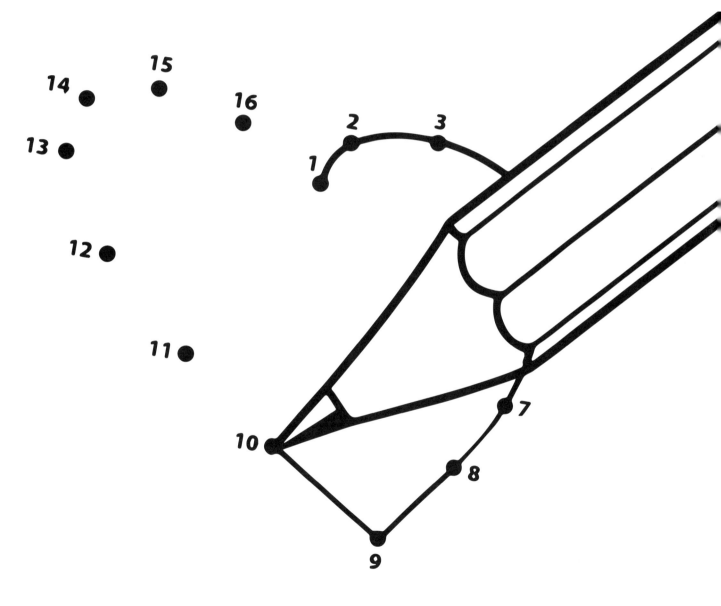

Prophets are Born
to Honk the Horn

God's people in the Old Testament were often like cars going the wrong way down a one-way street. Every now and then, God sent prophets to honk their horns and warn everyone to turn around. But most of the time, the prophets got run over. Then God's people were hurt very badly in major head-on crashes.

Everybody knows the **prophets** were a strange bunch that went against the flow of traffic, but their messages were on target and backed by the love of God. Each prophet showed how kind and willing God was to warn his people before He disciplined them.

Don't turn a deaf ear to the honks of God's Word. When you hear His warning, it's time to make a U-turn.

Amos 3:7 NLT

*Indeed, the Sovereign Lord never does anything until he reveals his plans to his servants the **prophets**.*

I Stick Like Glue
to What God Says to Do

God wants His Word to click and stick in our hearts. He shows parents how to make this happen by talking about His Word, day and night, as an all day, every day, way of life.

Did you ever **tie** a string around your finger, so you wouldn't forget something important? Well, God told His people to tie His commands to their hands, to wear them on their foreheads, and even to **stick** them on their doors and gates!

Likewise, HoneyWord Stick-ers will remind you of God's Word everywhere you go. And they'll help you stick like glue to what God says to do.

Deuteronomy 6:6-8 NLT

You must commit yourselves wholeheartedly to these commands that I am giving you today. Repeat them again and again to your children. Talk about them when you are at home and when you are on the road, when you are going to bed and when you are getting up. ***Tie*** *them to your hands and wear them on your forehead* ***as reminders****.*

I Can't Explain
but Prayer Can Break a Chain

Because of his great love for God, Peter was unfairly thrown in jail and chained between two soldiers. So the church prayed for his release.

Then, right in the middle of their prayer meeting, Peter himself knocked on the front door. The servant girl was so happy to hear his voice that she left Him outside behind the closed door. When she told everybody that God had answered their prayers, they all told her she was crazy.

You see, nobody can explain the power of prayer. Sometimes God answers quickly. Sometimes He seems to take forever. Other times He says no, so we think He didn't answer at all. But God wants us to know that our prayers always make a difference. Don't try to explain. Just pray and watch God break the **chains**.

Acts 12:6-7 NLT

*[Peter] was asleep, fastened with two **chains** between two soldiers. Others stood guard at the prison gate. Suddenly, there was a bright light in the cell, and an angel of the Lord stood before Peter. The angel struck him on the side to awaken him and said, "Quick! Get up!" And the **chains** fell off his wrists.*

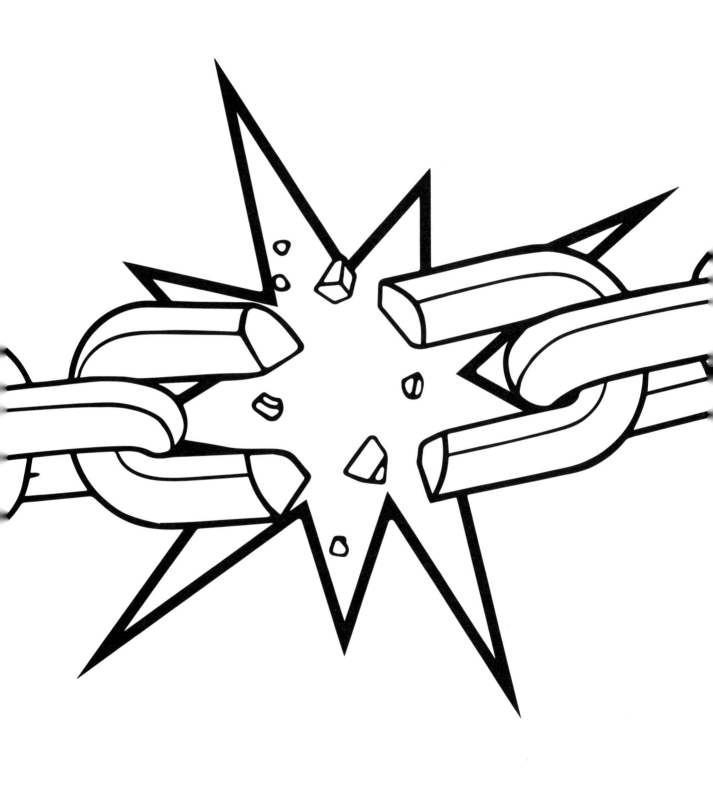

Lord, Give Me the Sense
to Stay Off the Fence

Fences are everywhere, and we're always on one side or the other. Joshua knew the same is true about friendship with God. Joshua wanted the people of Israel to stay on the Lord's side.

The choice was theirs. Joshua couldn't decide for them, and no one can **choose** for you either. Whose side are you on? It's the most important question you'll ever answer. You can't be on both sides of the fence at the same time.

If you're already on God's side, keep believing, trusting, and obeying. If you're on the other side, come on over. If you're trying to live on both sides, ask God for the sense to get off the fence. That's a prayer He loves to answer.

Joshua 24:15 NLT

*If you refuse to serve the Lord, then **choose** today whom you will serve. Would you prefer the gods your ancestors served beyond the Euphrates? Or will it be the gods of the Amorites in whose land you now live? But as for me and my family, we will serve the Lord.*

Jesus is My Friend
to The End

Most of us are pretty lousy friends. We shove our way to the front of the line. We serve ourselves the biggest cookies, and we wait for others to be friends with us first. But, as someone has wisely observed, "The only way to have a friend is to be one."

Well, Jesus knows how for sure. He is truly the best friend you'll ever have.

He came to earth so you could go to heaven. He became poor so you could become rich. He died so you could live. He was your friend, even while you were His enemy. And like a good movie, He promises to be your friend all the way to **The End**. No matter what!

Revelation 22:13 NLT
*"I am the Alpha and the Omega, the First and the Last, the Beginning and **The End**."*

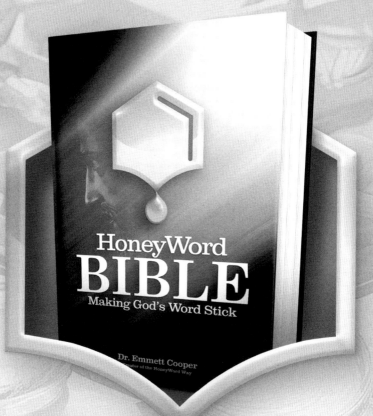

 HoneyWord.org

Visit HoneyWord.org for details.

28 Days To New Life
How Can I Apply What I Can't Remember?

Visit HoneyWord.org for details.

Learn all **52 Stick-ers**
while playing card games with

HoneyWord Click & Stick Playing Cards

Visit HoneyWord.org for details.

52 Stick-ers **Alphabetized**

Arrows 45	Knitted Sweater 55
Ball 35	Limb 87
Bloom 37	Nest 71
Boomerang 81	Orange Peel 65
Bread 43	Pizza 63
Brick Wall 89	Race Car 22
Bubbles 41	Rainbow 33
Candle 105	Red, Yellow, Black & White 39
Canoe 49	Rock 113
Cap 31	Seashell 59
Chain 123	Shoes 73
Compass 51	Skin 69
Crown 61	Soap 57
Cup of Water 103	Spider 99
Delete Button 115	Sponge 17
Dime 79	Submarine 85
Dot-to-Dot Picture 117	Sword 95
Dove 53	Table 67
Ears 77	The End 127
Fence 125	Trash 97
Flashlight 111	Treasure 93
Glue Stick 121	Turkey 29
Honey 75	TV 91
Horn 119	Vine 101
Kite 27	Woven Cloth 47
Knife 109	Yo-yo 83

 When God's Word clicks in my **"Click-er,"** 1

2 and I stick it to a **"Stick-er,"**

it ticks in my **"Tick-er"**
for a lifetime.